LETTER TRACING FOR KIDS
SEBASTIAN
TRACE MY NAME WORKBOOK

Can't Find Your Name?

Have our elves create a personalized book with the name of your choice today!

VISIT US AT:
PersonalizeThisBook.com

All rights reserved. No part of this book may be reproduced or transmitted in any form by any means, electronic or mechanical, including photocopying, scanning and recording, or by any information storage and retrieval system, without permission in writing from the publisher, except for the review for inclusion in a magazine , newpaper or broadcast.

Cover and page design by Cool Journals Studios - Copyright 2017

ABOUT ME

MY NAME IS:

Sebastian

I AM ☐ **YEARS OLD.**

I LIVE IN:

_____
- - - - - - - - - - -
_____

For parents

- - - - - - - - - - -
_____

For kids

DRAW YOU AND YOUR FAMILY

S

Sebastian

Sebastian

THIS IS HOW I WRITE MY NAME

MY NAME HAS ___ LETTERS

COLOR THE EGGS WITH LETTERS OF OUR NAME WRITE YOUR NAME

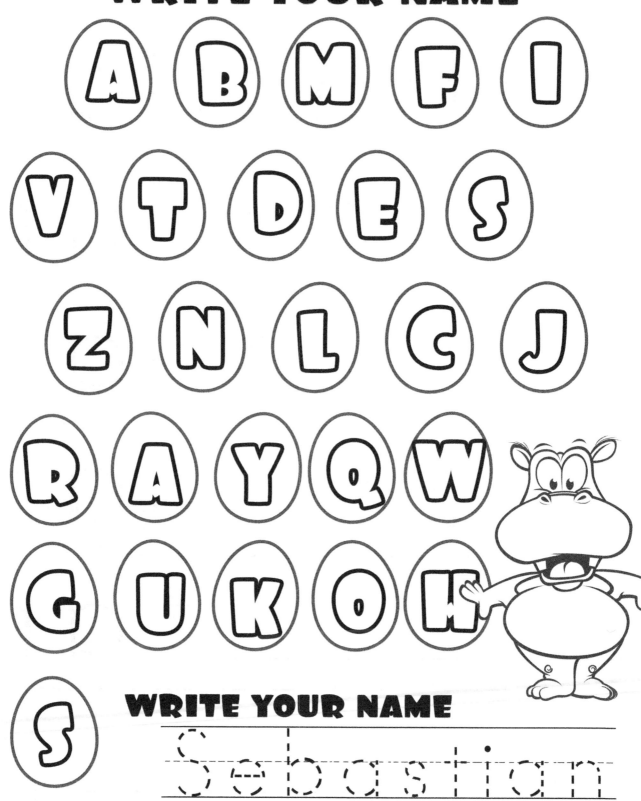

WRITE YOUR NAME

Sebastian

WRITE YOU NAME WITH,

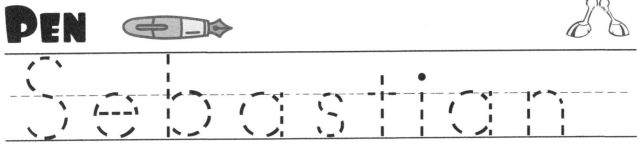

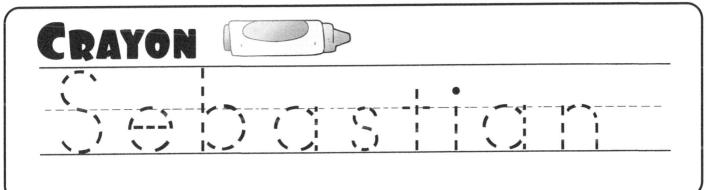

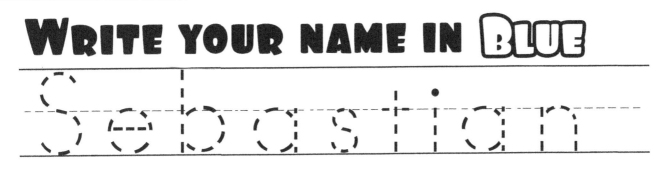

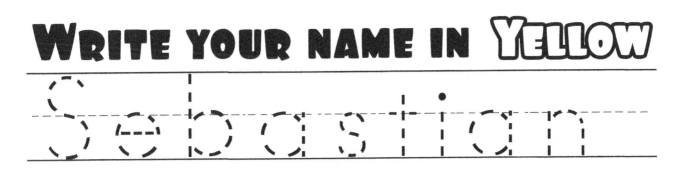

DRAW YOUR FAVORITE THINGS

COLOR

FOOD

TOY

ANIMAL

MY NAME

MY NAME STARTS WITH
_____

MY NAME ENDS WITH
_____

FILL THE LETTERS OF YOUR NAME WHITH DIFFERENT COLORS

S B W F V I T
D E S Z N L C
J R A Y Q K
G U A O H M

Sebastian

Sebastian

Sebastian

Sebastian

Sebastian

Sebastian

Sebastian

Sebastian

Sebastian

Sebastian

Sebastian

Sebastian

Sebastian

Sebastian

Sebastian

Sebastian

Sebastian

Sebastian

Sebastian

Sebastian

Sebastian

Sebastian

Sebastian

Sebastian

Sebastian

Sebastian

Sebastian

Sebastian

Sebastian

Sebastian

Sebastian

Sebastian

Sebastian

Sebastian

Sebastian

Sebastian

Sebastian

Sebastian

Sebastian

Sebastian

Sebastian

Sebastian

Sebastian

Sebastian

Sebastian

Sebastian

Sebastian

Sebastian

Sebastian

Sebastian

Sebastian

Sebastian

Sebastian

Sebastian

Sebastian

Sebastian

Sebastian

Sebastian

Sebastian

Sebastian

Sebastian

Sebastian

Sebastian

Sebastian

Sebastian

Sebastian

Sebastian

Sebastian

Sebastian

Sebastian

Sebastian

Sebastian

Sebastian

Sebastian

Sebastian

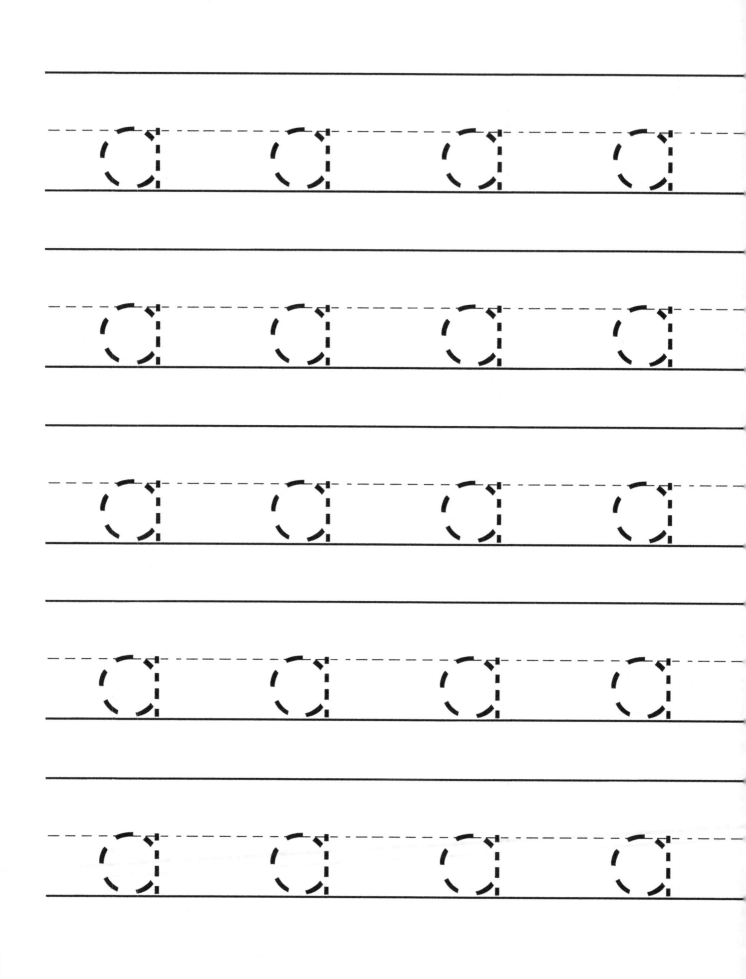

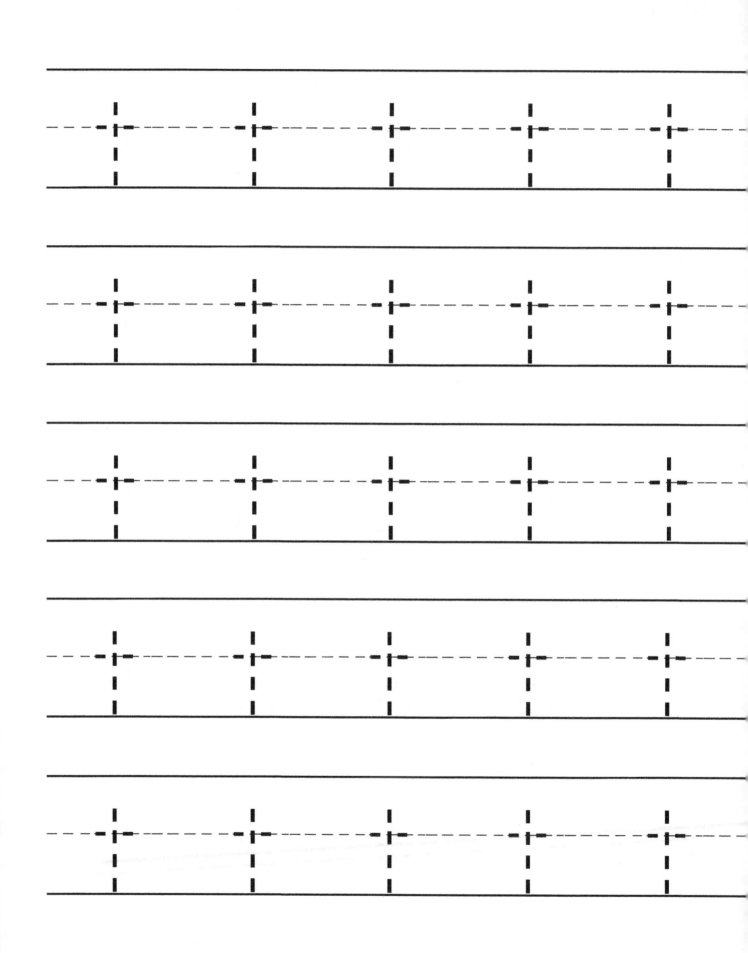

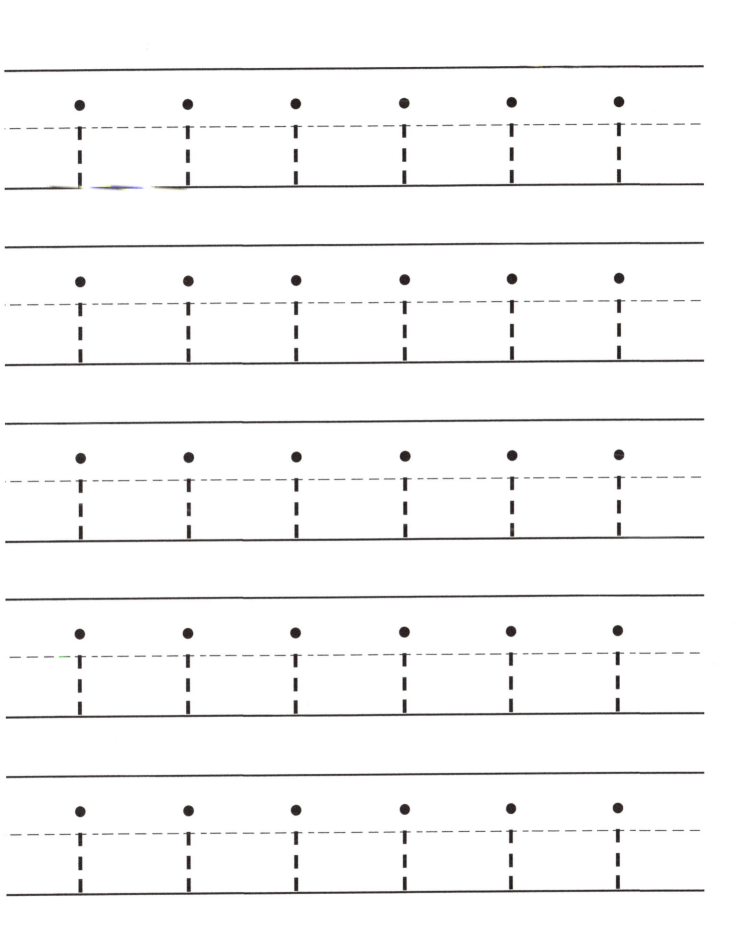

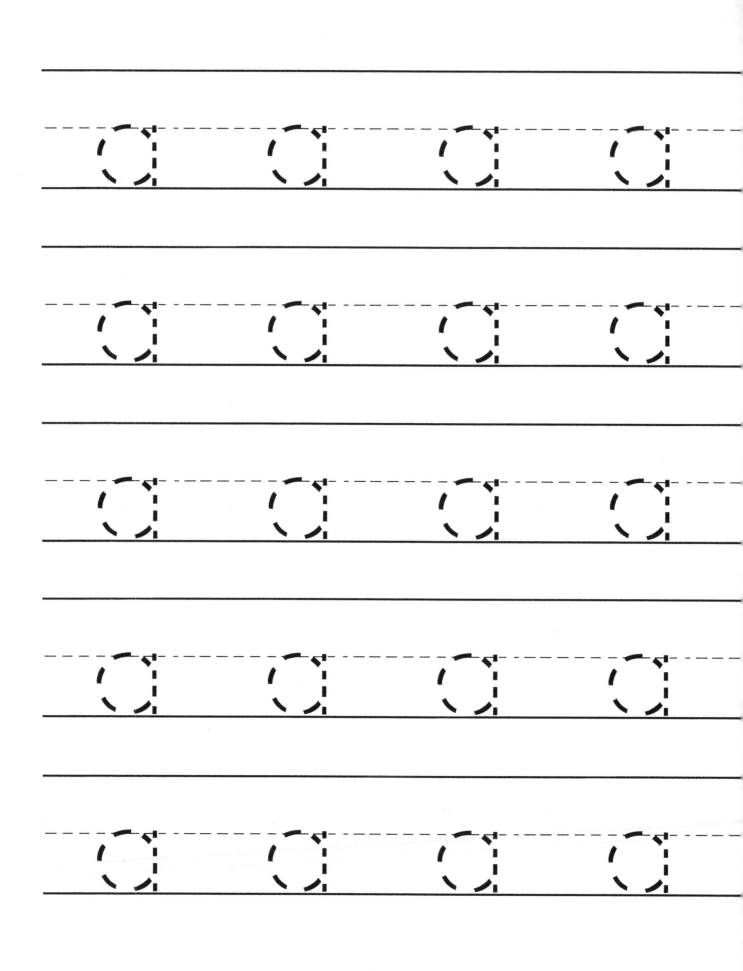

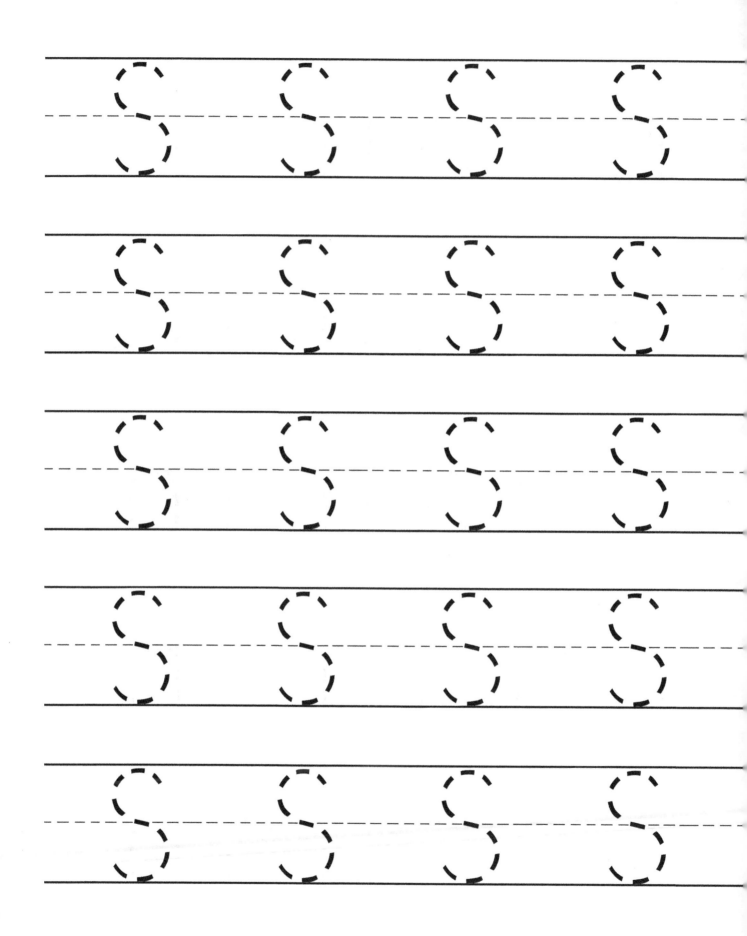

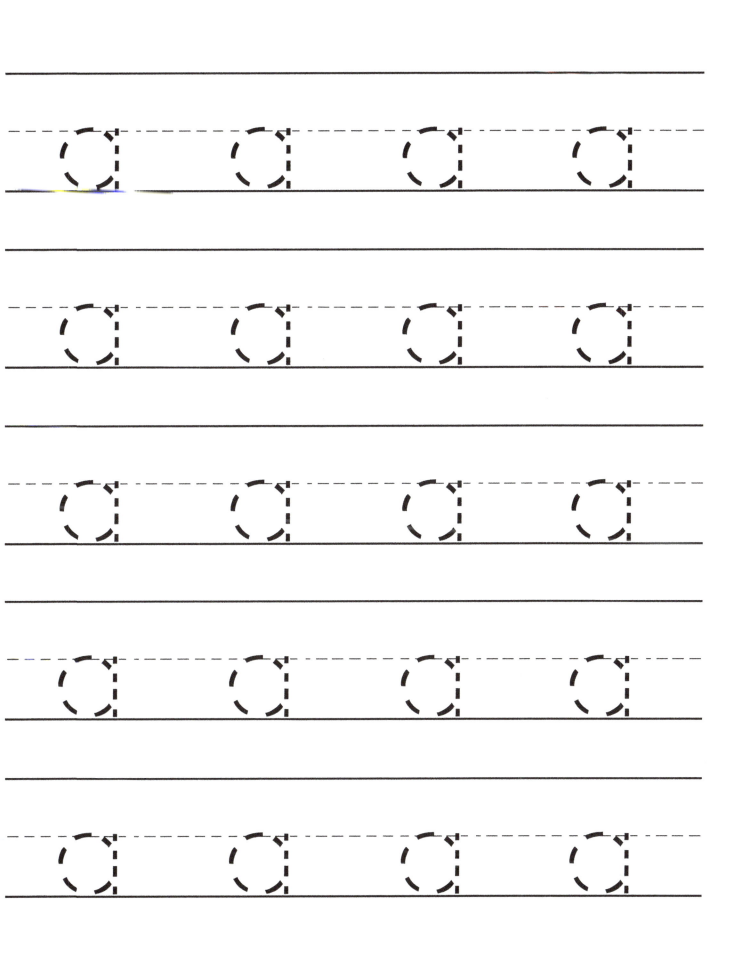

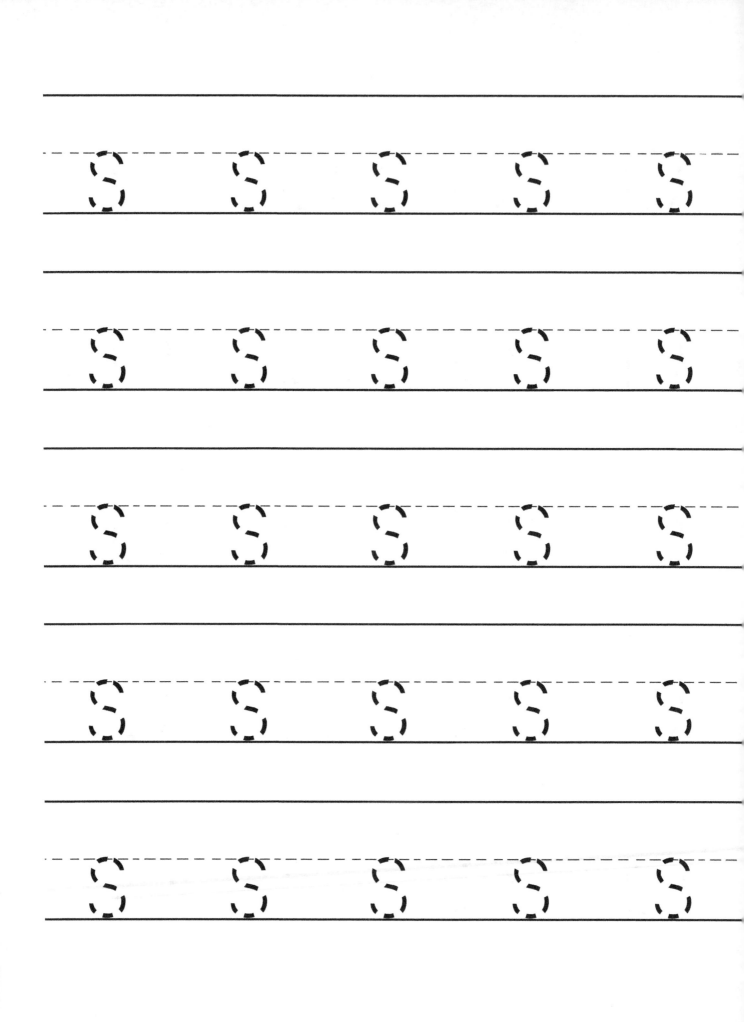

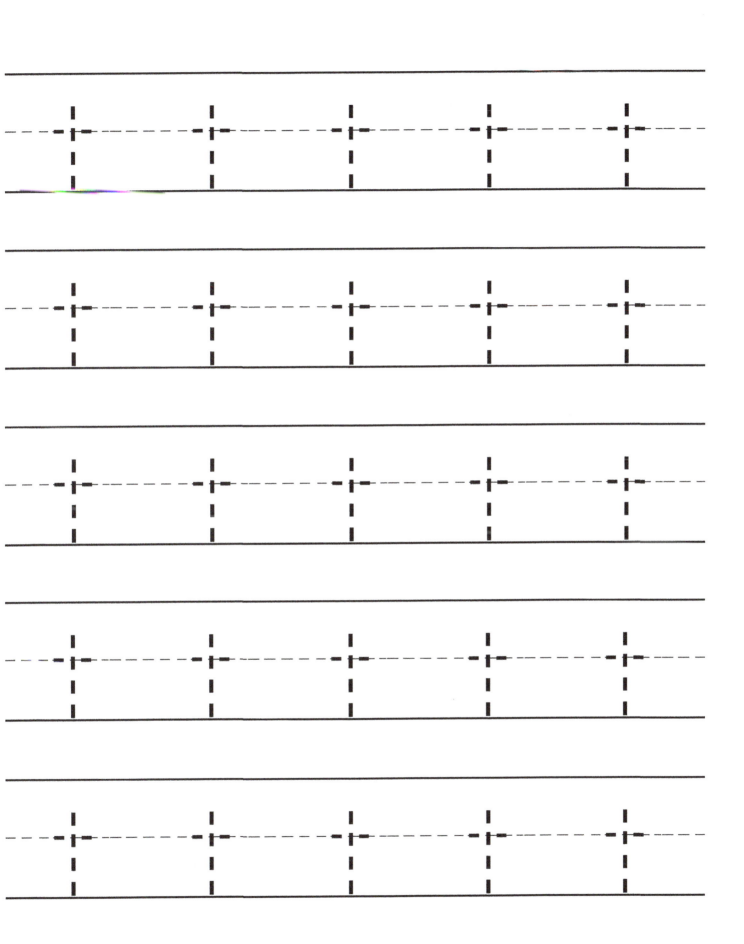

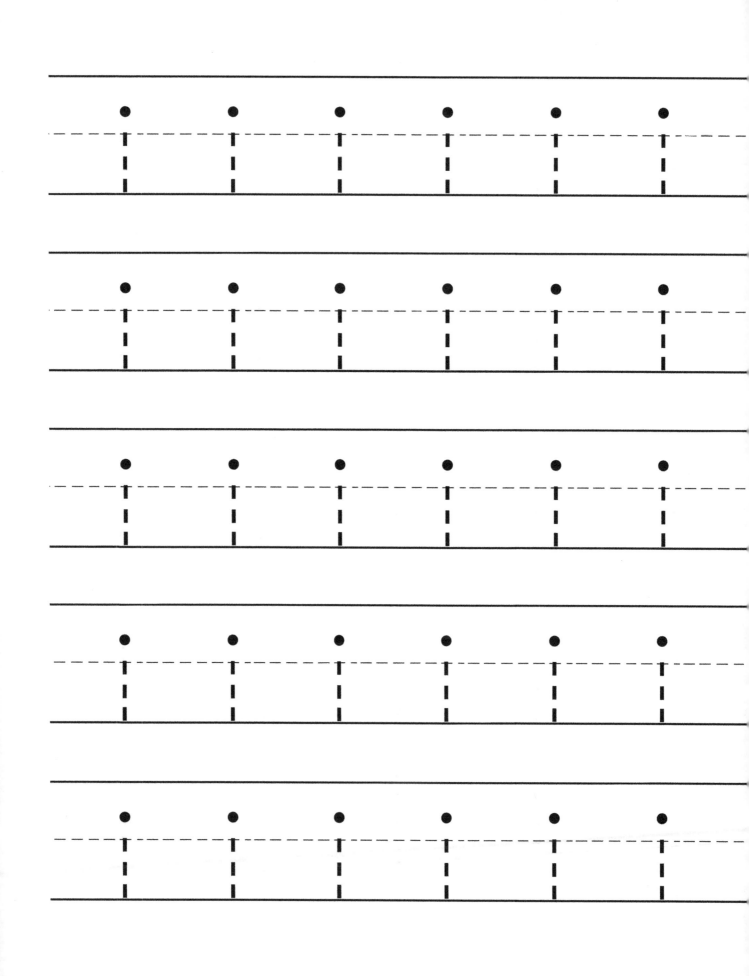

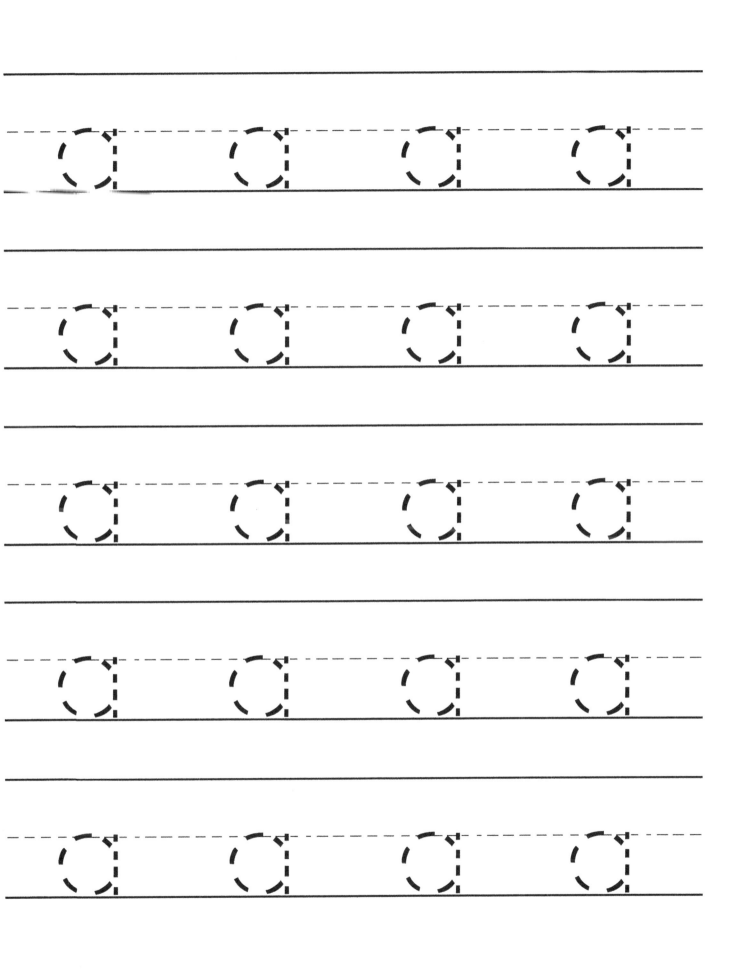

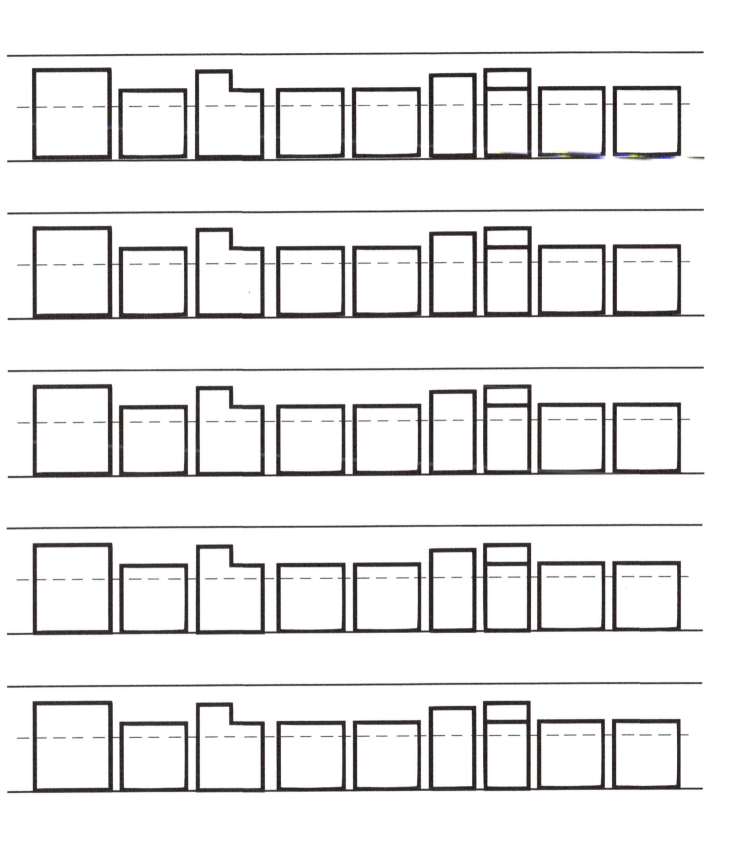

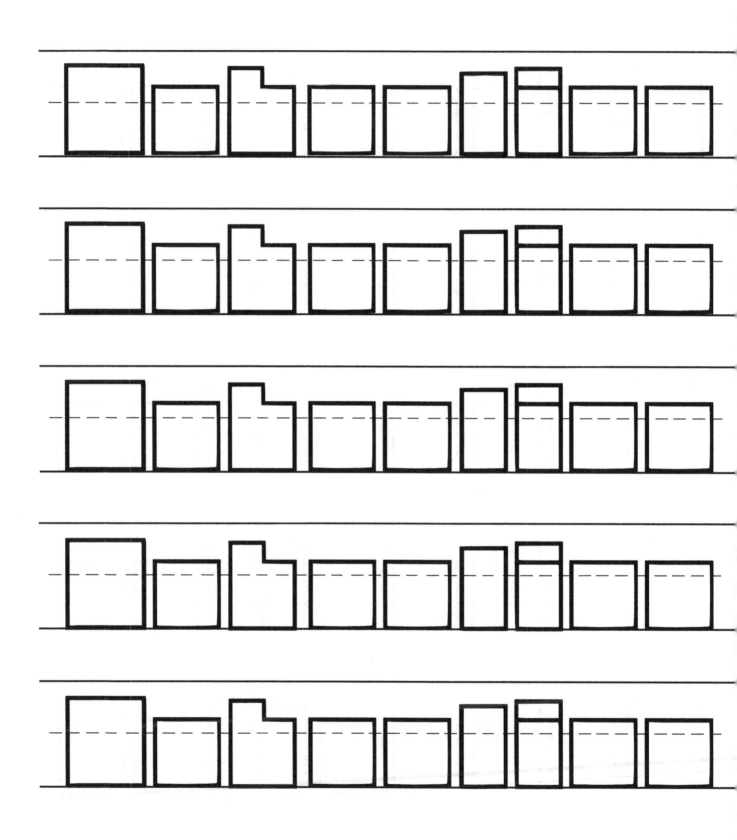

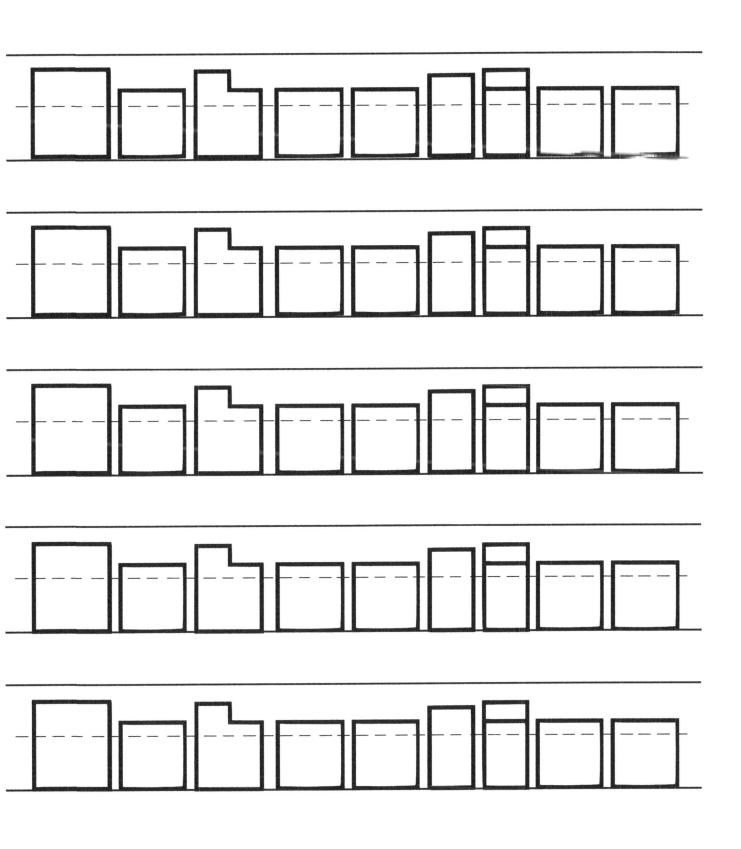

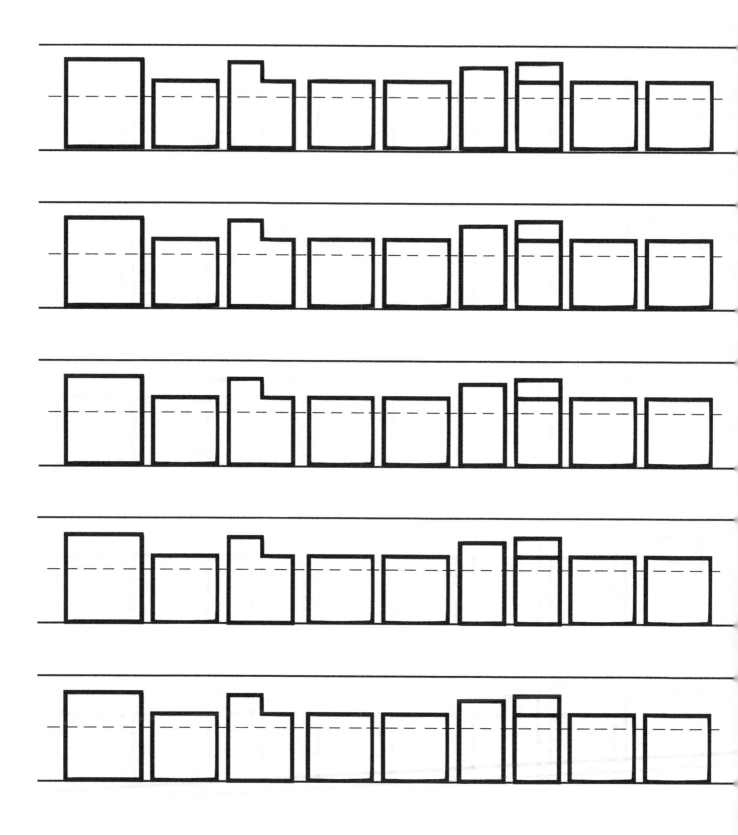

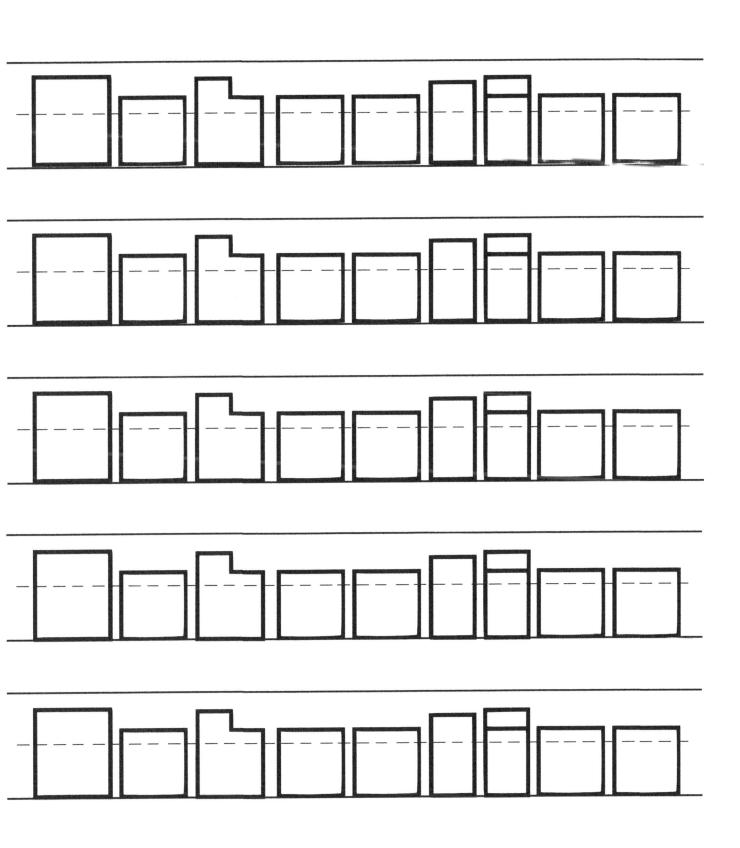

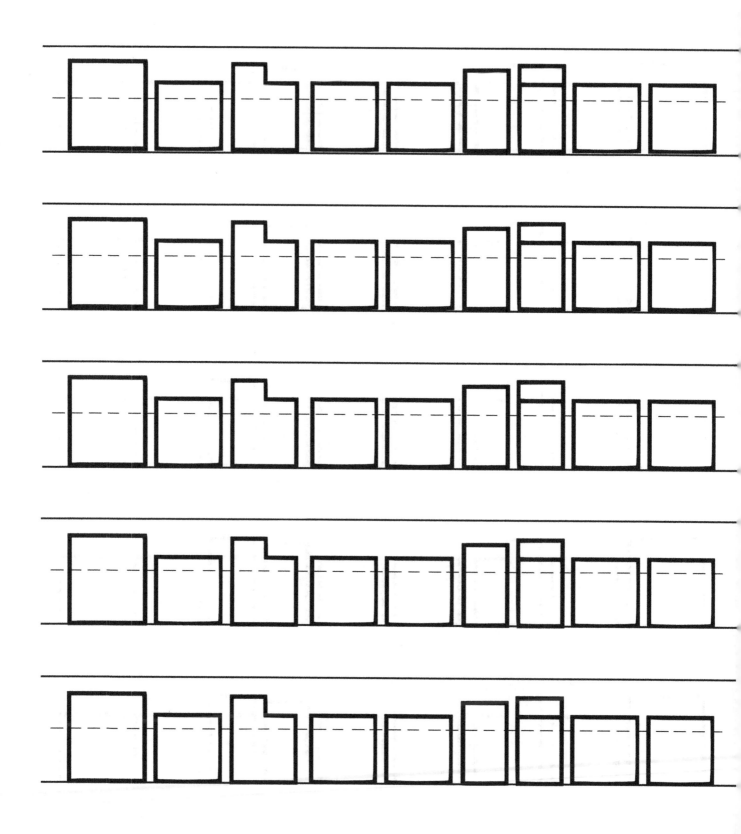

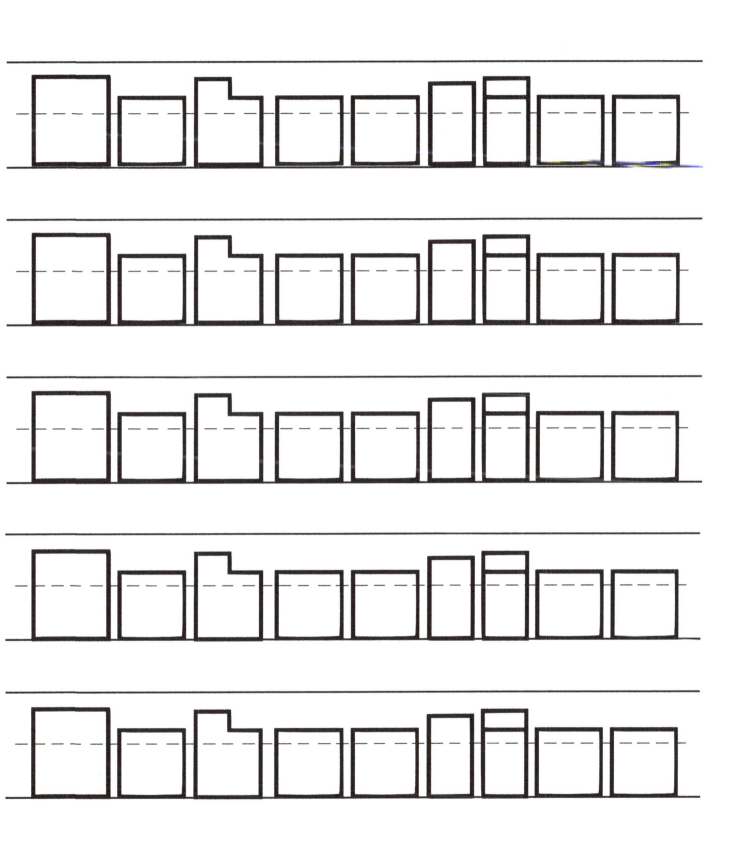

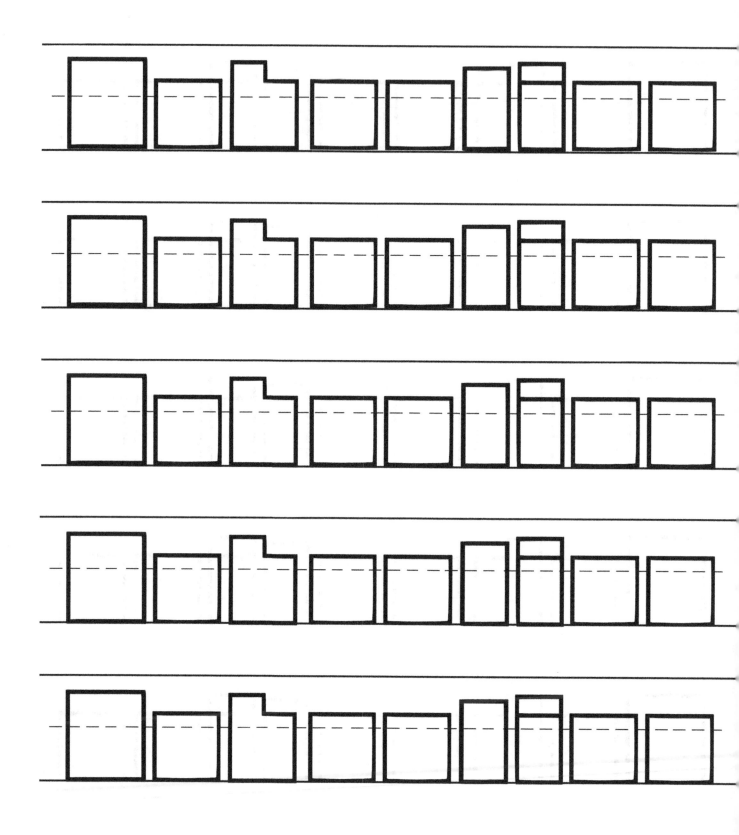

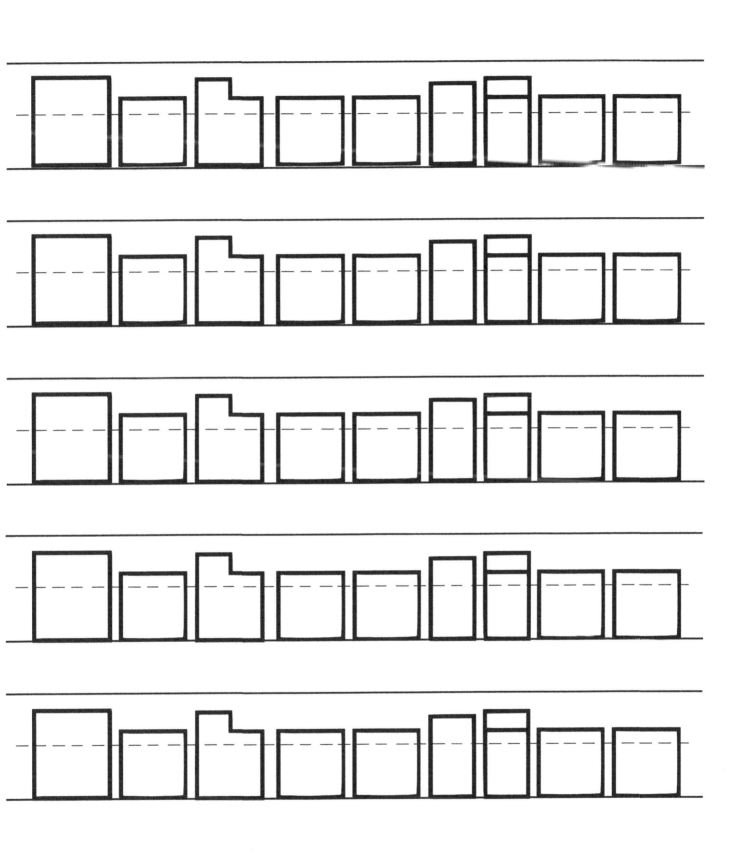

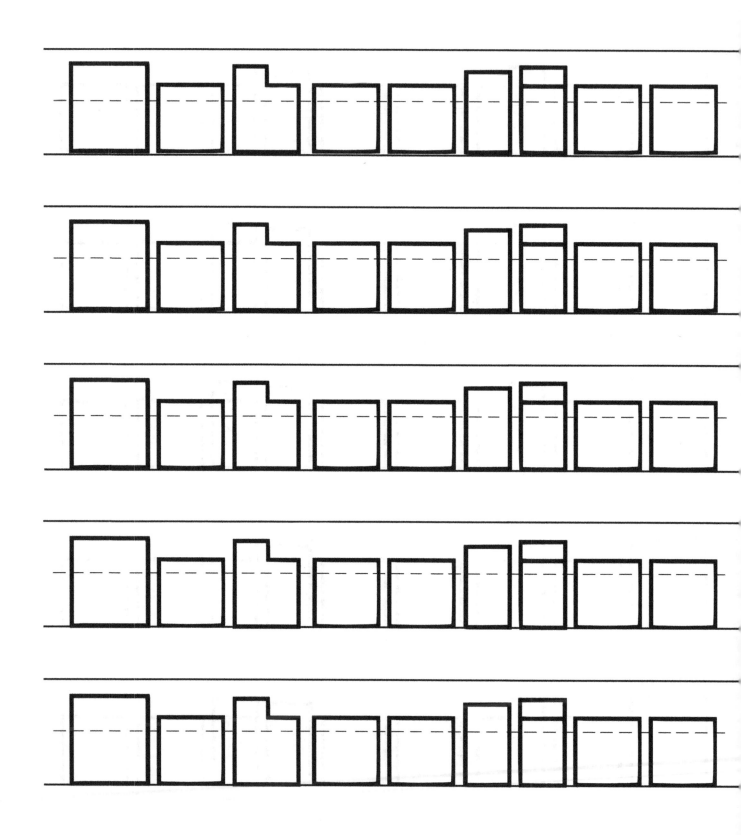

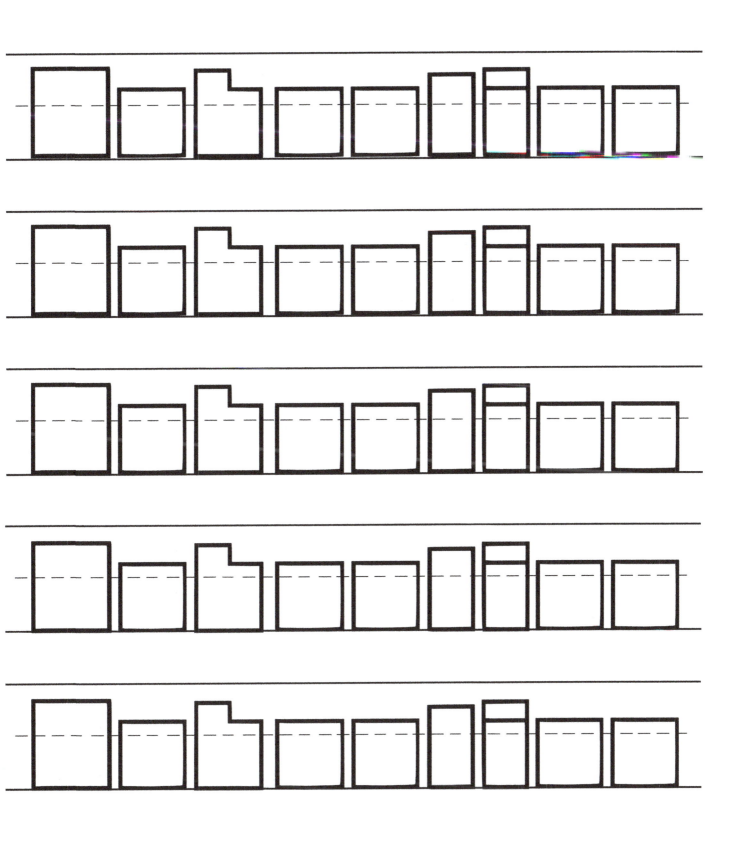

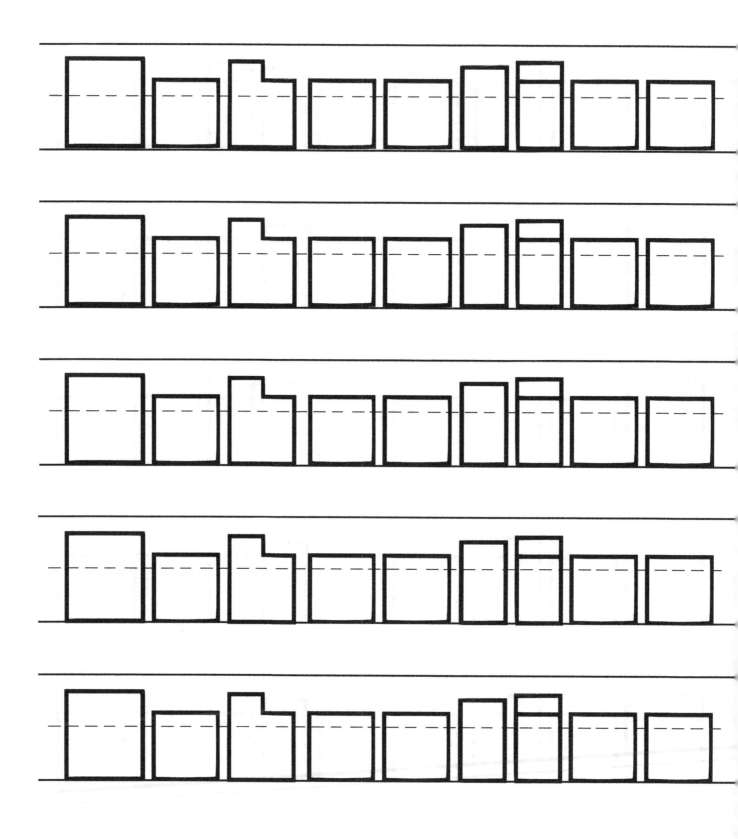

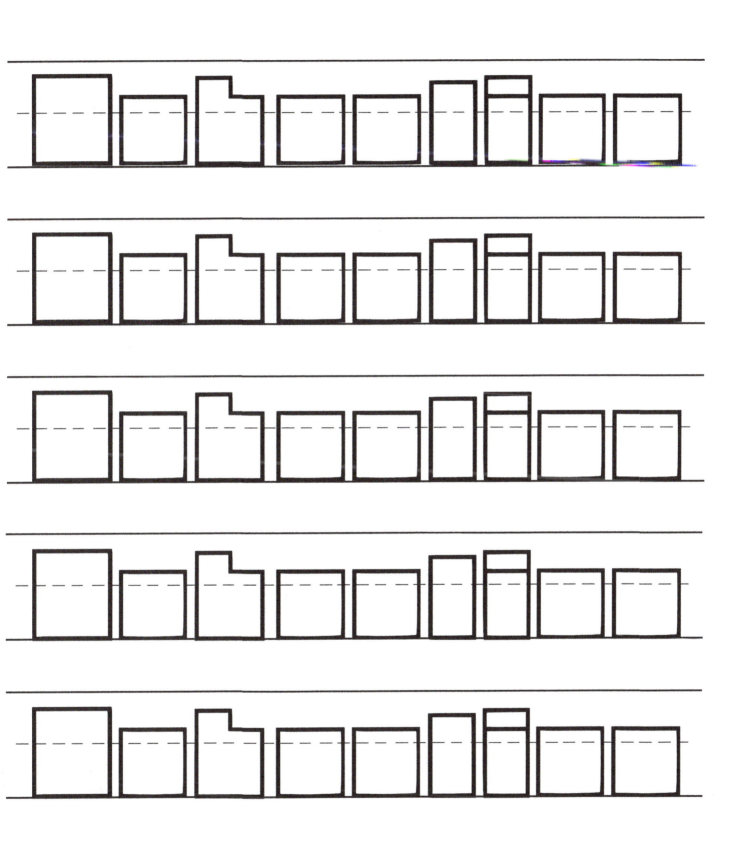

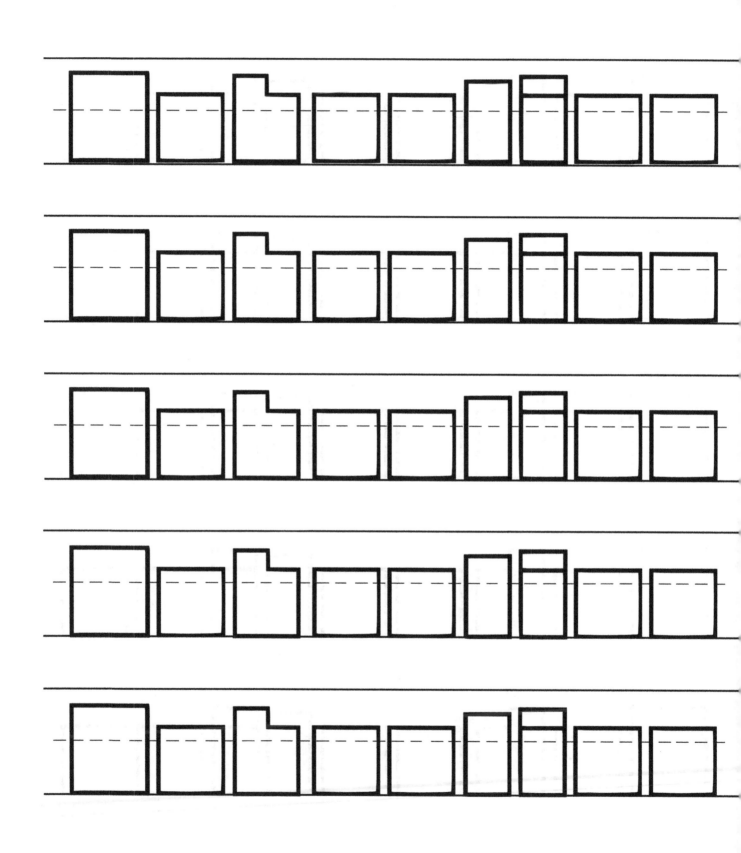

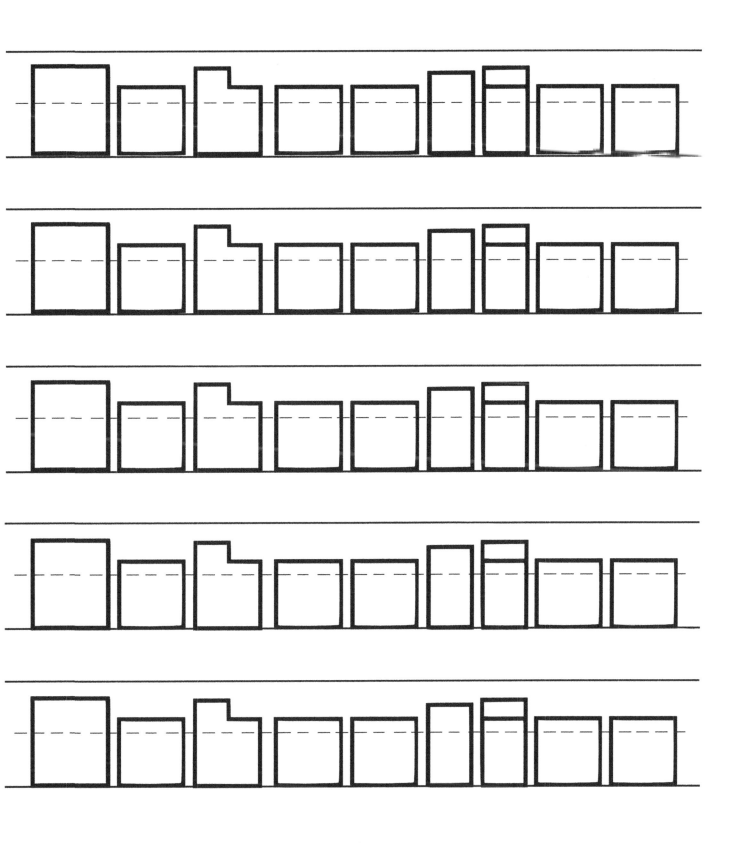

Sebastian

Sebastian

Sebastian

Sebastian

Sebastian

Sebastian

Sebastian

Sebastian

Sebastian

Sebastian

Sebastian

Sebastian

Sebastian

Sebastian

Sebastian

Sebastian

Sebastian

Sebastian

Sebastian

Sebastian

Sebastian

Sebastian

Sebastian

Sebastian

Sebastian

Sebastian

Sebastian

Sebastian

Sebastian

Sebastian

Sebastian

Sebastian

Sebastian

Sebastian

Sebastian

Sebastian

Sebastian

Sebastian

Sebastian

Sebastian

Sebastian

Made in the USA
Monee, IL
29 May 2022

97195580R00057